THE STORY OF
ROCK MUSIC

POP HISTORIES

MATT ANNISS

A+

Smart Apple Media

Published in the United States by Smart Apple Media
PO Box 3263, Mankato, Minnesota 56002

Text: Matt Anniss
Editors: Joe Harris and Rachel Blount
Design: Paul Myerscough and Keith Williams

Picture credits:
Corbis: Henry Diltz 14t, Douglas Kent Hall/ZUMA 11t, Hulton-Deutsch Collection 9b, 14b, Michael Ochs Archives 4, 17; Dreamstime: Imagecollect 15t; Flickr: Dave Smith 22; Shutterstock: Peter Albrektsen 16b, S Bukley 27c, Daniel DeSlover 28, Roxana Gonzalez 29t, Andreas Gradin 31, Northfoto 24, 27b, Keith Publicover 5, Nikola Spasenoski 21b, Ferenc Szelepcsenyi 23b, TDC Photography 15b, Shelly Wall 27t; Sony Music Entertainment 13b; Wikipedia: Stephanie D. 23t, Solly Darling 9t, Bill Ebbesen 7r, Mark Goff 12, Hydra Records/Klau Klettner 6, Jonathan King 21t, Heinrich Klaffs 18, Carl Lender 11b, Library of Congress 7l, Library of Congress/UPI 8, Music54 26, Helge Øverås 25t, Scott Penner 29b, Harry (Howard) Potts 20t, Rowland Scherman/USIA 10t, Jim Summaria 13t, W. W. Thaler/H. Weber/Hildesheim 10b, TheCuriousGnome 19, Urmelbeauftragter 16t, WikiPancu 20b, Xrayspx 1, 25b.
Cover images: Shutterstock: Harmony Gerber top left, s_bukley top center right, margo_black main, Nikola Spasenoski top center left, TDC Photography top far right; Wikipedia: Library of Congress top far left, Library of Congress/UPI top right.

Library of Congress Cataloging-in-Publication Data

Anniss, Matt.
 The story of rock music / Matt Anniss.
     pages cm. -- (Pop histories)
 Includes index.
 Summary: "Describes the beginnings and evolution of rock music, spotlighting important artists and songs"--Provided by publisher.
 ISBN 978-1-59920-969-2 (library binding)
 1. Rock music--History and criticism--Juvenile literature. I. Title.
 ML3534.A55 2014
 781.66--dc23
                              2013003612

Printed in China

SL002673US

Supplier 03, Date 0513, Print Run 2377

CONTENTS

BLUES ROOTS

Today, rock music is one of the most dominant forms of music on the planet. It has spawned many different styles, and its popularity shows no signs of waning. Yet rock is a relatively recent development. Its roots can be traced back to the African-American jazz and blues clubs of the 1930s.

Hard Times

In the early part of the twentieth century, life wasn't particularly great for most African Americans. While they were free of slavery, which had blighted the country up until 1865, laws still existed that effectively made them second-class citizens.

Musical Release

The escape for many African Americans was music. In backstreet bars, clubs, and music venues, a thriving black music scene developed. There, music that had its roots in the era of slavery was being updated for twentieth-century audiences.

IN 1958, R & B GROUP THE DRIFTERS RECORDED THE FIRST ROCK AND ROLL SONG TO FEATURE AN ORCHESTRA, THE TOP TEN HIT *THERE GOES MY BABY*.

Music from the Soul

The most influential of these styles was the blues. It featured raw, emotional performances of songs that reflected the harsh realities of life for African Americans. Many top blues performers, such as the traveling singer Robert Johnson, would later be celebrated as musical pioneers.

Rhythm Meets Blues

During the 1940s, the blues developed into "rhythm and blues" or R & B. By adding a backing band featuring drums, bass, piano, and occasionally saxophone, blues guitarists could make "rockin'" music to dance to.

GOING ELECTRIC

The blues scene was changed by the arrival of the electric guitar in the 1930s. This instrument would later become the backbone of rock music. The electric guitar sounded louder, harder, and fuzzier than the acoustic guitar.

PLAYLIST
ROCK AND ROLL ROOTS

Robert Johnson
—*Kind Hearted Woman Blues* [1936]

Lead Belly
—*Where Did You Sleep Last Night?* [1944]

Muddy Waters—*I Feel Like Going Home* [1948]

Howlin' Wolf—*Moanin' at Midnight* [1951]

Jackie Brenston & His Delta Cats—
Rocket 88 [1951]

Breakthrough Approaching

By the time the 1950s came around, young white musicians were beginning to pay attention to this exciting rhythm and blues sound. Soon, it would form the basis of a new style that would take the world by storm: rock and roll.

THE INVENTION OF THE MODERN ELECTRIC GUITAR HELPED GIVE ELECTRIC BLUES, ROCK AND ROLL, AND LATER, ROCK MUSIC THEIR DISTINCTIVE SOUNDS.

ROCK AND ROLL REVOLUTION

In the space of 10 years, rock and roll transformed the musical landscape, turning its top artists into the first global pop stars. A little-known style of African-American music had inspired a musical revolution.

Melting Pot

Although the roots of rock and roll lay in rhythm and blues, early songs featured influences from jazz, country, and folk music. Crucially, it was played and enjoyed by both black and white musicians.

CHICAGO SOUND

Rock and roll developed in several parts of the United States at the same time. Chess Records, based in Chicago, released some of the earliest rock and roll songs. They also gave the world one of rock and roll's first stars, Chuck Berry.

Star Performer

Chuck Berry gave energetic stage performances, played amazing riffs on his electric guitar, and sang about girls and cars. Like fellow black performers Fats Domino and Little Richard, he was as loud, brash, and fun as his songs. All three became huge celebrities.

Deep South

Meanwhile, down south in Memphis, Sun Studios was playing host to recording sessions from a good-looking young white trucker named Elvis Presley. In 1954, he recorded a song called *It's Alright Mama*. It was a big hit and turned Elvis into a huge star.

BRUCE SPRINGSTEEN ON ELVIS PRESLEY

"There have been a lot of tough guys. There have been pretenders. And there have been contenders. But there is only one king: Elvis."

Bruce Springsteen (pictured)

Rock Around the World

The song that really put rock and roll on the map was *Rock Around the Clock* by Bill Haley and the Comets. Featured in a 1955 movie called *Blackboard Jungle*, it went on to be one of the biggest selling songs of all time. Suddenly, rock and roll was big news around the world.

Global Sound

The success of artists such as Bill Haley, Elvis Presley, and Chuck Berry inspired teenagers on both sides of the Atlantic to buy guitars and start their own bands. For the next 20 years, musicians inspired by the rock and roll revolution would dominate the pop charts.

IN THE LATE 1950S, THE POPULARITY OF ROCK AND ROLL SINGERS WAS SO GREAT THAT THEY WERE OFTEN ASKED TO STAR IN THEIR OWN MOVIES, AS ELVIS PRESLEY DID IN 1957'S *JAILHOUSE ROCK*.

THE BRITISH INVASION

Although the United States was the birthplace of rhythm and blues and rock and roll, during the early 1960s the country leading the rock music revolution was Great Britain. From 1964 onward, its bands ruled the world.

Northern Lights

Britain had its own rock and roll scene from the late 1950s onward, but it wasn't until the early 1960s that its bands began to make an impact. At the time, the center of British rock music wasn't London but a port city in the North of England called Liverpool.

MERSEYBEAT

Up in Liverpool, a sound developed called "Merseybeat". It was a more radio-friendly version of rock and roll that sounded distinctly British. It retained key elements of rock and roll, such as rhythmic guitars and sturdy drumbeats, but sounded a lot more polished.

Meet the Beatles

The leading Merseybeat band was the Beatles. Made up of four identically dressed young friends with distinctive mop-top hairstyles, the Beatles enjoyed their first number one hit in 1963 and quickly went on to become the most popular band in the UK.

THE BEATLES LED A BRITISH MUSICAL "INVASION" OF AMERICA IN 1964. SHOWN HERE FROM LEFT TO RIGHT ARE JOHN LENNON, PAUL MCCARTNEY, GEORGE HARRISON, AND RINGO STARR.

Beatlemania

In February 1964, the Beatles made their first trip to the United States. Following an appearance on the *Ed Sullivan Show*, a popular TV variety show, they became huge news. Everywhere they went, the Beatles were followed by huge groups of screaming girls. By April, their songs occupied the top five positions on the Billboard Hot 100 chart.

LIAM GALLAGHER ON THE BEATLES
[OASIS]

"I'm not going to lie to you, I love the Beatles. They make me happy. I think they were the best and still are."

Liam Gallagher (pictured)

THE ROLLING STONES, SHOWN HERE IN 1965, ARE WIDELY CONSIDERED THE BEST ROCK BAND OF ALL TIME. THEY CONTINUE TO PLAY CONCERTS OVER 50 YEARS AFTER FIRST STEPPING ON STAGE IN LONDON.

From London with Love

In the wake of the Beatles' success, many other British bands became huge stars in America. Two bands from London with rhythm and blues roots, the Rolling Stones and The Who, enjoyed particularly big success. The press called it "the British invasion".

BRITISH SUCCESS

Over the next few years, British rock bands dominated the pop charts around the world. Newspapers and magazines were full of articles about "swinging London". The British had reinvented rock and roll.

OPEN YOUR MIND

By the mid 1960s, rock music was everywhere. The sound was going through a golden age. It was also changing, with bands all over the world pushing the boundaries and creating thrilling new styles.

Blues Revival

In Britain, groups such as Fleetwood Mac, the Yardbirds, and John Mayall's Blues Breakers were fusing rock with traditional American blues influences. In the United States, folk singers such as Bob Dylan and Joan Baez were picking up electric guitars and making "folk rock".

JOAN BAEZ AND BOB DYLAN TURNED TRADITIONAL FOLK MUSIC ON ITS HEAD BY PICKING UP ELECTRIC GUITARS AND CREATING A NEW STYLE CALLED FOLK ROCK.

Important Movement

The United States was also home to a distinct scene called "garage rock". This was less polished and well produced than other forms of rock music, but it proved to be quite influential on the way rock music developed in later years. Eventually, garage rock bands would influence the punk rock movement of the 1970s.

FLEETWOOD MAC'S PETER GREEN WAS ONE OF THE LEADING LIGHTS OF THE BRITISH BLUES-ROCK MOVEMENT DURING THE LATE 1960S.

MIND-ALTERING SUBSTANCES

During the mid-to-late 1960s, many things were changing. One was the emergence of dangerous, illegal, and mind-altering drugs such as LSD. Many rock musicians tried these drugs, and their music changed as a result.

Complex Songs

The Beatles, once clean-cut pop stars, decided to stop playing concerts. Instead, they spent a lot of time in recording studios making densely layered and highly inventive songs that could not easily be reproduced live.

Studio Revolution

The Beatles' 1967 album *Sergeant Pepper's Lonely Hearts Club Band* changed how rock bands made albums. Instead of capturing a single performance from a band, it featured "psychedelic rock" songs that used new recording techniques. For music fans used to listening to fairly simple songs, it was a revelation.

Hard Rock Roots

Another artist who changed the face of rock music was Jimi Hendrix. An American guitarist who lived in London, he recorded songs that featured amazing guitar solos over heavy beats and distorted chords. His sound became known as "hard rock" and would later inspire the development of "heavy metal".

JIMI HENDRIX'S MOST FAMOUS MOMENT CAME AT THE WOODSTOCK FESTIVAL IN 1969, WHERE HE FINISHED HIS SET WITH A HARD ROCK VERSION OF THE AMERICAN NATIONAL ANTHEM, *THE STAR SPANGLED BANNER*.

ROCK HEROES

FREDDY MERCURY ON JIMI HENDRIX

❝There's no way you can compare Jimi Hendrix to anyone else. You either have the magic or you don't. There's nobody who can take his place.❞

Freddy Mercury (pictured)

LIVING FOR THE WEEKEND

As the 1960s drew to a close, interest in rock music was higher than ever before. Because of this, some music enthusiasts decided to put on weekend-long events featuring some of their favorite bands. The music festival as we know it today was born.

WOODSTOCK, THE FIRST GREAT MUSIC FESTIVAL, ATTRACTED NEARLY HALF A MILLION ROCK AND ALTERNATIVE MUSIC FANS FROM ALL OVER AMERICA.

Fantasy Festival

The first music festivals weren't the work of business people looking to make money but rather people in America's underground rock music scene. Inspired by the great musical changes happening around them, they decided to put on a two-day celebration of rock in San Francisco.

Magic Music

The world's first-ever music festival took place in June 1967, in a San Francisco park. Called the Fantasy Fair & Magic Mountain Festival, it featured performances from Canned Heat, Captain Beefheart, and The Byrds. It marked the start of what has become known as rock music's "Summer of Love".

Trailblazers

Word of this amazing "rock festival" spread, and soon, events were popping up all over the world. The Miami Pop Festival took place in 1968 on a racetrack in Florida, while 10,000 people traveled to a small island off the south coast of England for the Isle of Wight Festival.

Legendary Event

The event that really put the rock music festival on the map was Woodstock in 1969. Held on farmland in New York state, it featured legendary performances from The Who, Sly and the Family Stone, Joan Baez, and Jefferson Airplane. It is estimated that over 500,000 people attended Woodstock, making it one of the biggest music festivals of all time.

MAKING HISTORY

The impact of these early weekend-long rock events was such that by 1970, rock festivals were an established part of the musical landscape. Over the years, they've gotten bigger and can now boast "headliners" from across the worlds of rock, pop, and dance.

LIVING LEGENDS

THE WHO

The original "festival band" was The Who. Famous for smashing up their instruments at the end of concerts, their loud, noisy, and energetic performances lit up many of the earliest music festivals. Since then, they've gone on to become rock legends and sell millions of albums.

SLY AND THE FAMILY STONE, A BAND THAT FUSED ROCK MUSIC WITH SOUL AND FUNK, WERE ONE OF THE HEADLINE ATTRACTIONS AT 1969'S LEGENDARY WOODSTOCK FESTIVAL.

13

GLAM IT UP

By the early 1970s, rock music was changing yet again. Bored by what they thought were the excesses of psychedelic rock, some musicians decided to go back to making no-frills rock music.

It's Only Rock and Roll

This wasn't a rock and roll revival, though. This new take on rock featured thumping beats, strong guitar riffs, and words that were easy to sing along to. It sat somewhere between pop music and hard rock.

MARC BOLAN, THE HUGELY TALENTED SINGER BEHIND THE POPULAR GLAM ROCK GROUP T. REX, WAS TRAGICALLY KILLED IN A CAR CRASH IN 1977.

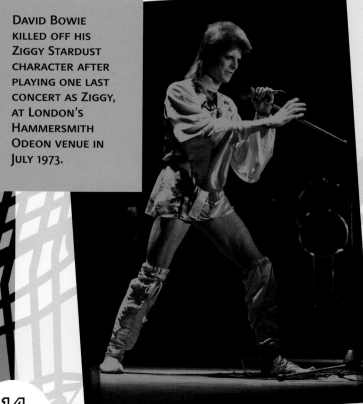

DAVID BOWIE KILLED OFF HIS ZIGGY STARDUST CHARACTER AFTER PLAYING ONE LAST CONCERT AS ZIGGY, AT LONDON'S HAMMERSMITH ODEON VENUE IN JULY 1973.

Glamorous Costumes

These new 1970s rockers also liked dressing up. For their performances, they dressed in outrageous clothes. Because of this, the music became known as "glam rock".

ZIGGY STARDUST

The man who did the most to put glam rock on the map was a British singer named David Bowie. He developed a character named Ziggy Stardust and became famous for wearing glittery costumes and makeup.

14

Glam Stars

David Bowie wasn't the only glam rock star. There was also Marc Bolan, the colorful singer behind the popular band T. Rex, and Bryan Ferry, the leader of an arty group called Roxy Music.

American Idols

Although many of the early glam rock stars were British, the sound soon began to become popular in America. The look and sound of David Bowie influenced many American artists, such as the New York Dolls, Iggy Pop, and Lou Reed.

The Birth of Punk

The New York Dolls were an important band. They developed a louder, simpler take on the sound called "glam punk". Their noisy style became the inspiration for punk rock, one of the most important musical movements of the 1970s.

DAVID BOWIE

Over the last 40 years, David Bowie has proved to be one of the most imaginative artists around. Famous for his ever-changing costumes and hairstyles, Bowie has recorded songs in many different styles, including glam rock, pop, disco, and drum and bass.

Glam Revival

Punk rock signaled the end for glam rock. However, its influence lives on. In the twenty-first century, artists such as the Killers, the Darkness, and Marilyn Manson have found fame on the back of a sound that borrows heavily from 1970s glam rock.

MODERN-DAY PERFORMERS SUCH AS MARILYN MANSON (PICTURED) REGULARLY BORROW SOUNDS, CLOTHES, AND STYLES FROM THE GLAM ROCK ERA.

PROGRESS

During the 1970s, glam rock stars didn't have it all their own way. Also wildly popular was progressive rock, a style that had grown out of the psychedelic rock movement of the late 1960s.

Serious Business

Progressive rock bands took themselves seriously. They thought that rock music should be about much more than fun songs and radio-friendly hits. At the heart of the progressive rock scene was the "concept album".

MIKE OLDFIELD'S INSTRUMENTAL "PROG ROCK" CONCEPT ALBUM *TUBULAR BELLS* WAS ONE OF THE BEST-SELLING RECORDS OF THE 1970S.

Say No to Singles

A concept album is a collection of songs or musical pieces connected by a common theme. Progressive rock bands liked concept albums because it freed them from the need to create short, catchy songs. They could put anything they liked on there, from long, drawn-out songs to tracks that featured no singing at all.

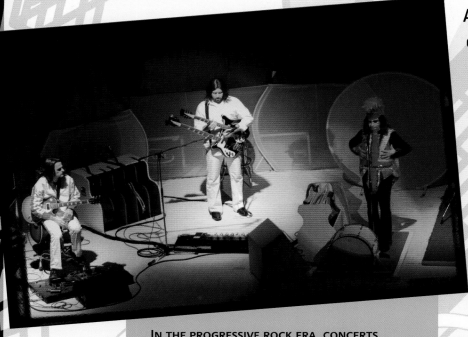

IN THE PROGRESSIVE ROCK ERA, CONCERTS BECAME LONGER AND MORE COMPLICATED, AS PERFORMERS TRIED TO ACCURATELY RECREATE THEIR LONG AND COMPLEX SONGS.

Music without Frontiers

One of the most popular progressive rock concept albums contained no singing at all. Mike Oldfield's *Tubular Bells* was designed to sound like a rock version of a classical music piece. To date, it has sold over 15 million copies worldwide.

DARK SIDE OF THE MOON

No progressive rock band released more concept albums than Pink Floyd. They became famous for making records full of epic tracks with long guitar solos. Their albums remain very popular with rock fans, and their most successful set, *Dark Side of the Moon*, has sold over 50 million copies.

Prog Superstars

During the heyday of progressive rock, there were many hugely successful bands. Genesis, Yes, Electric Light Orchestra (ELO), and the Moody Blues all enjoyed huge popularity on both sides of the Atlantic.

BRITISH BAND PINK FLOYD RECORDED A SUCCESSION OF HUGE-SELLING PROGRESSIVE ROCK ALBUMS DURING THE 1970S, INCLUDING *THE DARK SIDE OF THE MOON* (1973) AND *THE WALL* (1979).

PLAYLIST
PROGRESSIVE ROCK

Mike Oldfield—*Tubular Bells Part 1* (1973)

Genesis—*Firth of Fifth* (1973)

Camel—*Lady Fantasy* (1974)

Pink Floyd—*Shine on You Crazy Diamond, Parts 1–5* (1975)

Electric Light Orchestra—*Evil Woman* (1975)

Emerson, Lake & Palmer—*Fanfare for the Common Man* (1977)

On the Slide

Toward the tail end of the 1970s, the popularity of progressive rock began to wane. It was being overtaken not just by punk rock, but also by a new style that would go on to dominate the American rock scene: heavy metal.

GETTING HEAVY

Hard rock had been around since the late 1960s, but in the 1970s, it began to increase in popularity. Soon, the sound had a new name —heavy metal—and a huge following, particularly in the United States.

Whole Lotta Drums

The band that did the most to popularize hard rock in the early 1970s was Led Zeppelin. Their 1969 albums, *Led Zeppelin I and II*, took the popular British blues-rock sound and made it much heavier. Both albums were full of heavy drums, loud guitar riffs, and raw, noisy vocals.

Major Movement

Where Led Zeppelin led, others followed. During the early 1970s, bands such as Deep Purple, Grand Funk Railroad, UFO, Blue Oyster Cult, and Black Sabbath all released albums that further defined the ear-splitting hard rock sound.

AMERICAN METAL

Heavy metal, as it was soon known, was particularly popular in the United States. There, two bands emerged in the first half of the 1970s that would go on to become huge global stars: Aerosmith and Kiss.

WITH THEIR LOUD BLUES-ROCK RIFFS AND EVEN LOUDER VOCALS, LED ZEPPELIN INSPIRED A WHOLE GENERATION OF BANDS TO MAKE HARD ROCK MUSIC.

Grassroots Movement

Music reviewers didn't like heavy metal, and it barely got any coverage in the media. Yet that didn't stop the sound from becoming the dominant form of rock music in America. Metal fans were extremely dedicated and would flock to concerts in huge numbers.

Punk Inspiration

Inspired by the raw, fast sound of punk rock, a new breed of heavy metal acts began to appear in the late 1970s. As the original pioneers of the sound began to fade, metal fans turned to the fast new sounds of Motorhead and Iron Maiden.

International Breakthrough

As the 1970s drew to a close, heavy metal was on the verge of a major international breakthrough. With famed guitarist Eddie Van Halen at the forefront, metal would go on to spearhead a new era of "stadium rock".

INSIDE THE SOUND
HEAVY METAL

Heavy metal is deliberately louder and more powerful than other forms of rock music. It is characterized by long, drawn-out guitar chords, heavy basslines, and pounding drums, often played at high speed. Heavy metal singers often scream or wail for added effect.

HEAVY METAL BAND AEROSMITH EMERGED IN THE 1970S. DURING THE 1980S, THEY WOULD GO ON TO BE PIONEERS OF THE STADIUM METAL MOVEMENT.

STADIUM ROCK!

During the 1980s, rock, and particularly heavy metal, enjoyed a commercial boom. While it rarely reached the singles chart, its popularity was such that its biggest stars could tour the world and play to huge audiences.

Heavy Success

At the start of the decade, heavy metal was easily the most dominant form of rock music on the planet. Eddie Van Halen, Aerosmith, and Kiss became household names, while new bands such as Def Leppard and Iron Maiden took America by storm.

IRON MAIDEN SPEARHEADED A NEW WAVE OF BRITISH HEAVY METAL DURING THE EARLY 1980S, BEFORE BECOMING ONE OF THE WORLD'S MOST POPULAR STADIUM METAL BANDS.

Metal Milestone

The popularity of heavy metal was so big that by 1984, 20 percent of all albums sold in the United States were by heavy metal bands. This popularity allowed top metal bands to head out on huge concert tours where they would perform to sports stadiums full of fans.

Glam Metal Heroes

Among the most popular rock bands were those who put on theatrical performances. Glam metal bands such as Poison and Cinderella became just as famous for their crazy outfits and onstage antics as for their loud and crass records.

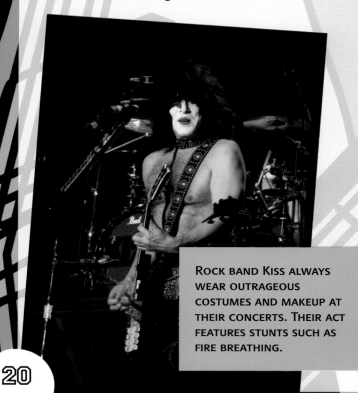

ROCK BAND KISS ALWAYS WEAR OUTRAGEOUS COSTUMES AND MAKEUP AT THEIR CONCERTS. THEIR ACT FEATURES STUNTS SUCH AS FIRE BREATHING.

NEW BREED

Toward the tail end of the 1980s, two bands emerged who would go on to become genuine international rock stars. Both Jon Bon Jovi and Guns N' Roses were not standard metal bands. Instead, they mixed metal with traditional hard rock.

Legends of Stadium Rock

It wasn't just metal bands enjoying success on the stadium rock circuit, either. Rhythm and blues stalwarts the Rolling Stones were still a huge draw, while new rock bands, such as U2, were beginning to fill arenas.

Still Popular

The stadium rock revolution of the 1980s set a trend for huge global concert tours that still continues to this day. Now, the world's most popular rock bands can make hundreds of millions of dollars every year just from playing concerts.

JON BON JOVI BECAME AN ALMOST OVERNIGHT STADIUM ROCK SENSATION DURING THE 1980S.

LIVING LEGENDS

GUNS N' ROSES

Since forming in 1985, Guns N' Roses have gone on to dominate the hard rock and heavy metal scenes, selling in excess of 100 million albums. Still active, they are famous for their "hard partying" attitude and record-breaking tours. Between 1991 and 1993, they played an astonishing 194 concerts in 27 different countries.

ALTERNATIVE ROCK

While the world's biggest metal and rock bands were smashing up hotel rooms and playing to huge audiences all over the world, another scene was taking shape. Away from the gaze of the media and most music fans, an alternative rock revolution was taking place.

Different Sounds

In a sense, alternative rock is just as old as rock itself. Alternative literally means "different", and over the years, the name has been used to describe many different musical styles. In fact, many styles that eventually became popular—such as rock and roll, rhythm and blues, and metal, were once deemed "alternative".

Alternative History

In the 1960s, garage rock was alternative. In the 1970s, that honor fell to punk rock and, in the early days, heavy metal. All three styles eventually found their way into the mainstream in one way or another, like all the best alternative music styles.

Indie Means Independent

During the 1980s, the alternative rock style was built on the underground success of the independent rock scene. This was built around tiny independent record labels that would release music from interesting new bands.

IT WAS ONLY WHEN ALTERNATIVE ROCK BANDS EARNED MAINSTREAM SUCCESS IN THE 1980S THAT GROUPS SUCH AS SONIC YOUTH FINALLY FOUND FAME.

School of Rock

With the support of college radio stations aimed at university students, a thriving underground "college rock" scene developed during the 1980s. Here, alternative rock bands could play to audiences of up to a couple of thousand a night, building their reputations.

PLAYLIST
ALTERNATIVE ROCK

New Order—*Ceremony* (1981)

REM—*Radio Free Europe* (1983)

Husker Du—*Celebrated Summer* (1985)

Sonic Youth—*Expressway to Yr. Skull* (Madonna, Sean, and Me) (1986)

Pixies—*Where Is My Mind* (1988)

Nine Inch Nails—*Head Like a Hole* (1989)

THE PIXIES WERE ONE OF THE FIRST AMERICAN ALTERNATIVE ROCK BANDS TO FIND FAME ON THE OTHER SIDE OF THE ATLANTIC, BECOMING DARLINGS OF THE BRITISH INDIE-ROCK SCENE.

Breeding Ground

To this day, the underground alternative rock circuit continues to be a breeding ground for top rock bands. As we will discover, it helped launch the careers of a string of bands that would dominate the rock scene in the 1990s and beyond.

FAMOUS FACES

Some very famous bands first made their name on the alternative college rock circuit. REM, Sonic Youth, and Nine Inch Nails all earned their stripes playing to small crowds on college campuses.

WITH THEIR LOVE OF "INDUSTRIAL" DANCE MUSIC AND HARD ROCK, TRENT REZNOR'S NINE INCH NAILS WERE ONE OF THE MOST INTERESTING ALTERNATIVE ROCK BANDS OF THE 1980S AND 1990S.

CHANGING OF THE GUARD

In the 1990s, the alternative rock and indie-rock scenes rose in prominence. By the middle of the decade, bands once considered alternative were now able to fill huge stadiums and arenas.

Grunge

The trend that started it all was "grunge", a loose and fuzzy style originally inspired by 1960s garage rock. It was developed in the city of Seattle by bands signed to the Sub Pop record label. The biggest stars of grunge were Nirvana.

ANTIHEROES

Led by charismatic but troubled frontman Kurt Cobain, Nirvana lived up to rock's "antihero" label. They dressed scruffily, made difficult rock music, and didn't care whether or not they were successful.

Huge Record Sales

Yet Nirvana were hugely successful. The band's 1991 album *Nevermind* went on to sell 30 million copies. Over the coming years, American alternative rock and British indie-pop would dominate the global rock scene.

In-Demand Band

The two biggest stadium rock bands of the time were two former alternative rock acts from the 1980s. The undisputed leaders were REM, whose albums *Automatic for the People* (1992) and *Monster* (1993) turned them into the most in-demand band on the planet.

A NEW BREED OF ALTERNATIVE ROCK BANDS (SUCH AS REM, PICTURED HERE) MADE THE LEAP TO STADIUM ROCK DURING THE 1990S.

From Me to U2

Not far behind was an Irish band from Dublin called U2. They had already built up a big following by the end of the 1980s, but during the '90s their popularity rocketed. It was the 1991 album *Achtung Baby* and subsequent *Zoo TV* world tour that saw U2 confirm their status as kings of stadium rock.

Amazing Show

For *Zoo TV*, U2 only played in enormous venues and surrounded the stage with fireworks and huge video screens. The tour set the standard for all future stadium rock shows. It also capped the relentless rise of alternative rock.

LIVING LEGENDS

U2

U2 got their big break in 1978, when they won a "battle of the bands" competition in their hometown of Dublin, Ireland. During the 1980s, they steadily built up a cult following before finally making it big in the 1990s. They currently hold the Guinness World Record for the most successful world tour of all time, earning $376 million in ticket sales between 2009 and 2011.

IRISH BAND U2 HAD BEEN AROUND SINCE THE LATE 1970S, BUT THEY FINALLY ACHIEVED STADIUM ROCK HERO STATUS DURING THE 1990S.

LOOKING BACK TO LOOK FORWARD

Like many musicians, rock bands often look to the sounds of the past for inspiration. Since 2000, rock's past has returned in a big way, with both new and old bands mining the sounds of the 1960s, '70s, and '80s.

Coming Around Again

Looking to the past for inspiration is not a new thing. Many of the alternative rock bands of the 1980s were fans of garage rock, while Merseybeat and 1960s British pop were the driving force behind the 1990s Britpop explosion.

THANKS TO THEIR ENERGETIC LIVE SHOWS AND A SOUND THAT SITS SOMEWHERE BETWEEN POST-PUNK AND THE ROLLING STONES, THE BLACK KEYS ARE ONE OF THE HOTTEST BANDS OF THE EARLY TWENTY-FIRST CENTURY.

New for Old

Since the 2000s, the rock scene has been dominated by bands that sound like they come from another era. There were the Killers and the Darkness and their take on glam rock, Arcade Fire and Kings of Leon with their vintage alternative rock sound, and the emo punk-rock of Jimmy Eat World.

POST-PUNK REVIVAL

Another sound that has proved popular is post-punk alternative rock, a style first made famous in the 1980s. Franz Ferdinand, the White Stripes, the Strokes, and Black Rebel Motorcycle Club all found fame playing songs that sounded like classic post-punk.

Keys Are Good

In recent years, one of the hottest bands around has been The Black Keys. The American duo emerged from the underground with a style that sits somewhere between post-punk and the classic rhythm and blues of the Rolling Stones.

Classic Rock

The popularity of bands that base their style on old rock sounds has also increased interest in classic rock bands from many years ago. This has led to many old bands getting back together to tour, particularly those from the 1960s and 1970s.

ROCK HEROES

JON BON JOVI ON THE ROLLING STONES

"The Rolling Stones set the bar as to what a rock band should be. But I don't envision myself touring in the way they do—my knees won't hold out."

Jon Bon Jovi (pictured)

IN 2012, THE ROLLING STONES RETURNED TO THEIR HOMETOWN OF LONDON TO PERFORM A SERIES OF SELLOUT SHOWS AT THE O2 ARENA.

IN THE 2000S, BANDS SUCH AS QUEENS OF THE STONE AGE BECAME BIG STARS ON THE BACK OF A SOUND THAT BORROWED HEAVILY FROM 1970S HARD ROCK.

Old Gold

Two of the most popular classic rock acts still touring are the Rolling Stones and The Who. Despite recording their best material nearly 40 years ago, both bands are still capable of filling huge arenas. This is because their music appeals to young and old rock fans.

IT'S ALL ROCK

Rock music has come a long way since the first rock and roll records emerged from Chicago and Memphis in the early 1950s. It has provided entertainment to millions of people and given us some of the most remarkable bands of all time.

Alive and Kicking

In the twenty-first century, rock music is in great shape. The live music scene, the backbone of rock, is more popular than it has been since the 1960s. From tiny backstreet bars to enormous sports stadiums, live rock music is everywhere.

Rock Star Games

The continuing popularity of rock music has even inspired some top-selling computer games. The Rock Band and Guitar Hero series of games, which allow wannabe musicians to play along with their favorite hits, have proved hugely popular.

Classic rock bands, from the Rolling Stones and The Who to Genesis and UFO, continue to tour and play to enormous audiences. The Rolling Stones have been performing now for almost 60 years, and in October 2012, they announced a series of concerts which sold out in record time.

Nothing Changes

Heavy metal is generally ignored by the media but still has a massive following. The boundaries between alternative and mainstream rock continue to be blurred, with new bands making the leap from small venues to huge arenas every year.

MANY FAMOUS ROCK GROUPS, SUCH AS ALTERNATIVE HEROES SOUNDGARDEN (PICTURED), GET BACK TOGETHER MANY YEARS AFTER SPLITTING UP, IN ORDER TO SATISFY THE DEMAND FROM FANS FOR LIVE CONCERTS.

New Forms

Beyond the mainstream, rock music continues to be taken in different directions by experimental bands. The last decade has seen a rise in "rock-tronica", a fusion of rock music and electronic dance music. Oslo, Norway, is home to a number of musicians that produce music that fuses progressive rock and dance music.

Rock On!

Rock music refuses to die. It's been entertaining music fans for nearly 70 years and will continue to do so for many years to come. It's only rock and roll ... but we love it!

FORMER WHITE STRIPES MAN JACK WHITE HAS RECORDED SOME OF THE EARLY TWENTY-FIRST CENTURY'S MOST EXCITING MODERN ROCK SONGS.

● PLAYLIST
MODERN ROCK

Wolfmother—*New Moon Rising* (2009)
LCD Soundsystem—*Someone Great* (2009)
The Black Keys—*Tighten Up* (2011)
Green Day—*Oh Love!* (2012)
Jack White—*Freedom at 21* (2012)

GLOSSARY

alternative Different.

commercial Mainstream, popular, something that sells well.

crass Crude or simple.

defined Identified, explained, or made clear.

distinct Unique, like nothing else around.

drawn out Stretched out, long.

epic Exceptionally long or large.

folk-rock A style of music that mixes traditional folk-style songs with rock guitars, drums, and bass.

global Worldwide.

inspiration Something that makes people excited enough to do similar things, for example, a particular song, band, or style of music.

jazz A popular style of music developed by African Americans in the late nineteenth and early twentieth centuries.

mainstream Popular and well-known.

pioneers People who did something first, such as playing a new style of music.

post-punk A style of rock music that came after punk rock.

psychedelic rock A strange style of rock music, often influenced by the use of illegal drugs.

punk rock A loud, noisy, fast, and simple style of alternative rock that first emerged in the 1970s.

record (or vinyl record) A pressed plastic disc featuring recorded music. The forerunner of the CD.

record label A company that specializes in recording and manufacturing music on record, CD, or digital download.

recording studio The place where musicians gather together to record their songs, prior to release on record, CD, or download.

revolution A big event that changes something forever, for example, music.

theatrical Something that looks like it belongs in a theater.

tour A series of concerts in different towns or cities, played in sequence.

underground Little-known, popular with a small number of people.

FURTHER INFORMATION

Further Reading

Even More Rock Family Trees by Pete Frame (Omnibus Press, 2011)

The History of Rock by Steven Rosen (Crabtree, 2009)

Play It Loud!: The Rebellious History of Music by Sara Gilbert (Compass Point Books, 2010)

The Rolling Stones: The Greatest Rock Band by Heather Miller (Enslow, 2010)

Web Sites

http://www.altpress.com
Alternative Press *is a great source for all the latest on the music of alternative rock musicians and bands.*

http://www.digitaldreamdoor.com/ pages/best_songs-Alternative.html
Listen to the 100 greatest and most influential alternative rock tracks of all time on this web site.

http://www.rockhall.com
Find out more about the history of rock music and the musicians who inspired today's greatest bands at The Rock and Roll Hall of Fame and Museum web site. With photos, videos, and more.

http://www.rollingstone.com
Check out America's number one rock music magazine on the Internet, featuring videos, news, interviews, and more.

http://www.spin.com
This magazine has been championing rock music in its many forms since 1985.

INDEX